# Journey Through Space
# The Planets

NEPTUNE

URANUS

SATURN

JUPITER

MARS

THE SUN

EARTH

VENUS

MERCURY

# Chelsea Donaldson

## Crabtree Publishing Company
www.crabtreebooks.com

**Author:** Chelsea Donaldson
**Publishing plan research and development:**
Sean Charlebois, Reagan Miller
Crabtree Publishing Company
**Project development:** Clarity Content Services
**Project management:** Clarity Content Services
**Editors:** Kristi Lindsay, Wendy Scavuzzo
**Copy editor:** Dimitra Chronopoulos
**Proofreader:** Kathy Middleton
**Design:** First Image
**Cover design:** Samara Parent
**Photo research:** Linda Tanaka
**Production coordinator:** Ken Wright
**Prepress technician:** Ken Wright
**Print coordinator:** Katherine Berti

**Photographs:**
NASA: p5 lower, 8, 9, 15, 17, 20 lower; top vectomart/
shutterstock: p5; Hemera/Thinkstock: p7; Hemera/
Thinkstock: p10; JPL/NASA: p11 (top); Hemera/
Thinkstock: p11 (bottom); Revenant/shutterstock: p12;
De Mango/shutterstock: p13 (top); Hemera/Thinkstock:
p13 (bottom); Digital Vision/Thinkstock: p14; JPL/
University of Arizona/NASA: p16; Lunar and Planetary
Institute/NASA: p18; JPL/NASA: p19; Space Telescope
Science Institute/NASA: p20 (top); Aaron Rutten/
shutterstock: p21; HomeArt/shutterstock: background;
© Eileen Hart/iStockphoto: front cover (boy); Jurgen
Ziewe/shutterstock: front cover (planets); Thinkstock:
back cover

---

**Library and Archives Canada Cataloguing in Publication**

Donaldson, Chelsea, 1959-
The planets / Chelsea Donaldson.

(Journey through space)
Includes index.
Issued also in electronic format.
ISBN 978-0-7787-5307-0 (bound).--ISBN 978-0-7787-5312-4 (pbk.)

1. Planets--Juvenile literature. I. Title. II. Series: Journey
through space (St. Catharines, Ont.)

QB602.D65 2012       j523.4       C2012-901246-7

**Library of Congress Cataloging-in-Publication Data**

CIP available at Library of Congress

---

# Crabtree Publishing Company
www.crabtreebooks.com      1-800-387-7650

Printed in the U.S.A./032012/CJ20120215

**Published in Canada**
Crabtree Publishing
616 Welland Ave.
St. Catharines, Ontario
L2M 5V6

**Published in the United States**
Crabtree Publishing
PMB 59051
350 Fifth Avenue, 59th Floor
New York, New York 10118

**Published in the United Kingdom**
Crabtree Publishing
Maritime House
Basin Road North, Hove
BN41 1WR

**Published in Australia**
Crabtree Publishing
3 Charles Street
Coburg North
VIC 3058

# The Planets

What Is a Planet? 4

How Do Planets Move? 6

Mercury 8

Venus 10

Earth 12

Mars 14

Jupiter 16

Saturn 18

Uranus and Neptune 20

Planet Facts 21

Learning More 22

Glossary 23

Index 24

# What Is a Planet?

You know that Earth is a **planet**. But do you know what makes it a planet? A planet
- travels around a star, such as our Sun;
- is a sphere;
- has **gravity** that is strong enough to move other objects out of its path.

Earth is all of these things!

Other objects travel around our Sun, too. Are they planets?
- **Asteroids** are space rocks. They come in many shapes, not just spheres. Are they planets? No!
- **Dwarf planets** are spheres. Their gravity is too weak to keep other objects out of their paths. Are they planets? No!

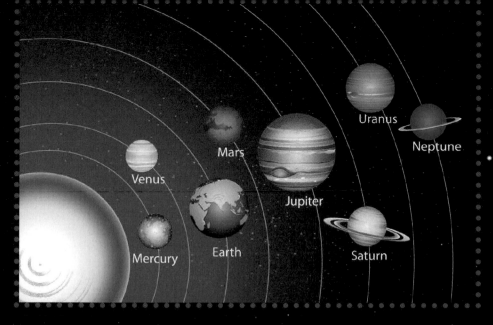

Eight planets travel around the Sun in our **solar system**. The lines in this diagram show the path each planet follows.

Uranus

Neptune

Mars

Venus

Jupiter

Mercury

Earth

Saturn

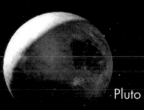

Pluto

Pluto was a planet until 2006. Scientists decided it was only a dwarf planet because it's gravity was too weak.

# How Do Planets Move?

Planets in our solar system **orbit**, or travel around, the Sun. Each planet takes a different path in its orbit. One complete orbit is one year. We call this type of movement a **revolution**.

As each planet orbits, it also **rotates**, or spins, on an **axis**. An axis is an imaginary line through the middle of the planet from its top to its bottom. It takes Earth one day, or 24 hours, to make one complete rotation. Some planets have shorter days, so they have shorter rotations. Other planets' rotations are much longer. What would life be like if the Sun only rose every seven months, like the way it does on Venus?

Sun

Mercury

Venus

Earth

Mars

Jupiter

Saturn

Uranus

Neptune

# ACTIVITY: Move Like a Planet!

## What You Will Need
- a Styrofoam ball (planet)
- a needle and thread
- a lamp (the Sun)

## Steps

**Step 1:** Ask an adult to thread a needle and push it into the ball as far as it will go.

**Step 2:** Hold the thread so the planet can spin.

**Step 3:** Hold the planet about four inches (10 cm) from a lamp and watch it spin. See how only one side of the planet gets the Sun's light. The side closest to the Sun has day. The side away from the Sun has night.

**Step 4:** Now, walk around the Sun in a circle. Keep your planet spinning! Each circle is one year.

## What Happens?
What happens if you walk in a larger circle around the Sun?

# Mercury

Mercury is the smallest planet. It is the same size as Earth's moon. You could fit 18 planets the size of Mercury inside Earth. Like the Moon, Mercury is covered in holes called **craters**.

Mercury is close to the Sun, so its days are very hot. Most things would burst into flame there, including you! At night, however, it becomes extremely cold. Mercury rotates very slowly. One of Mercury's days is about as long as two of Earth's months. That is a long day!

Mercury has a short year, too. It orbits the Sun in just 88 Earth days.

These four planets, Mercury, Venus, Earth, and Mars, are all made of rock.

Scientists think comets and meteors made craters when they crashed into Mercury.

# Venus

Next to Mercury is Venus. Venus is very bright. It is easy for us to spot since Earth and Venus are neighbors. You do not even need a **telescope**, although it helps. The best time to look for Venus is at sunrise or sunset.

In this picture, Venus is the bright dot beside the Moon.

Venus and Earth are almost the same size. Both have large, flat areas and high mountains. But Venus and Earth are also very different. Venus is the hottest planet in the solar system! It has volcanoes 100 times bigger than Earth's volcanoes. Clouds of acid float through the air there. Lightning storms light up the sky. Venus also rotates in the opposite direction that Earth rotates.

Venus is the
second planet
from the Sun.

Telescopes make
faraway things look
closer and larger.

11

# Earth

From space, Earth looks blue because a large part of the planet is covered in oceans. Earth also has air we can breathe and a mild climate. It is a perfect place for living things. No other planet in our solar system is like Earth.

Earth rotates on an angle. In winter, the **northern hemisphere**, or the top half of Earth, tilts, or leans, away from the Sun. That makes that part of Earth colder. In summer, the northern hemisphere tilts toward the Sun. That part of Earth then warms up. What do you think happens in the **southern hemisphere**, or the bottom half of Earth, when it is winter in the top half?

A moon is a solid object that orbits a planet. Earth has only one moon. Some planets have hundreds!

Earth takes one year to revolve around the Sun. As Earth moves around the Sun, it also rotates on an angle. This angle puts different parts of Earth closer to the Sun at different times. That is what creates the different seasons.

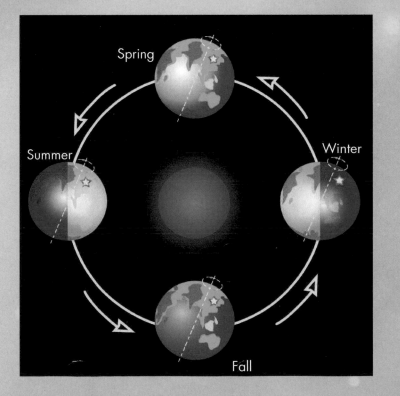

Spring

Summer

Winter

Fall

# Mars

Some people call Mars the Red Planet. Why? The planet is covered in red dust. Mars looks like a desert today. Some lines on its surface look like dried-up lakes and rivers. Scientists think there may be a large frozen sea under parts of its surface. Perhaps a long time ago it had water, like there is on Earth.

Did life ever exist on Mars? Does it still exist, deep under the ground? No one knows! Scientists are planning to send people to Mars. It would take six to eight months to get there. Would you like to travel to Mars?

Can you see the area that looks like a dried-up river?

# Jupiter

Beyond Mars are the planets made up of **gases**: Jupiter, Saturn, Uranus, and Neptune. If you stepped on one of these planets, your foot would go right through!

You could fit more than 1,000 Earths into Jupiter. It is by far the largest planet in our solar system. It also has more than 60 moons.

This planet is very stormy. One storm looks like a big red spot. It has been blowing for over 300 years!

This giant red spot is a storm on Jupiter. The red spot is three times larger than Earth!

# Saturn

Saturn is the beauty of the solar system. It has rings that are made of dust and rocks. These rocks are left over from a small moon that broke apart long ago.

The surface of Saturn is striped. It has bands of gases, mainly hydrogen, methane, and helium. These gases are very light. In fact, if Saturn were in water instead of space it would float!

The *Cassini* spacecraft has been exploring Saturn since 2004. So far, it has found more than 60 moons! Some of them may be able to support life.

The *Cassini* spacecraft is still out there exploring Saturn.

# Uranus and Neptune

Pale blue Uranus is eight times bigger than Earth. It has hundreds of moons. Scientists think Uranus once crashed into something really big. The whole planet is tipped on its side! Uranus also rotates in the opposite direction that Earth rotates.

Neptune is the farthest planet from the Sun. It takes 165 Earth years to complete one orbit. Neptune's surface is very cold. But deep under the ground, it is hotter than the Sun. The heat from below rises to the cold surface. That causes wild storms and winds.

# Planet Facts

Here are some facts about the planets in our solar system. Which one would you most like to visit?

| | How wide? | One day is about... | One year is about... |
|---|---|---|---|
| **Mercury** | 3,032 miles (4,880 km) | 59 Earth days | 88 Earth days (about 3 months) |
| **Venus** | 7,521 miles (12,104 km) | -243 Earth days | -225 Earth days (about -7 months) |
| **Earth** | 7,918 miles (12,743 km) | 1 Earth day | 365 1/2 Earth days |
| **Mars** | 4,212 miles (6,779 km) | 24 1/2 Earth hours | 687 Earth days (22 1/2 months) |
| **Jupiter** | 86,881 miles (139,821 km) | 10 Earth hours | 12 Earth years |
| **Saturn** | 72,367 miles (160,463 km) | 10 ½ Earth hours | 29 Earth years |
| **Uranus** | 31,518 miles (50,723 km) | -17 Earth hours | -84 Earth years |
| **Neptune** | 30,559 miles (49,244 km) | 16 Earth hours | 165 Earth years |

**Note:** The negative symbol ( - ) means the planet rotates and revolves in the opposite direction than that of Earth.

# Learning More

WEBSITES

**www.nasakids.com**

Visit NASA Kids' Club for challenging space games and to learn about the latest information about space.

**http://starchild.gsfc.nasa.gov/docs/StarChild/ StarChild.html**

StarChild is a learning center for young astronomers. Created by NASA, this website offers exciting images and activities.

**www.kidsastronomy.com/solar_system.htm**

This website has information about the different planets in our solar system.

OTHER BOOKS

**The Stars**
**The Sun**
**The Moon**

# Glossary

**asteroids** Space rocks

**axis** (AK-sihs) An imaginary straight line through an object around which it spins

**craters** (KRAY-turz) Holes caused by objects hitting the surface of a planet or moon

**dwarf planets** Objects that revolve around the Sun, like a planet, but do not have enough gravity to be a planet

**gravity** (GRA-vih-tee) The force of attraction between matter

**northern hemisphere** (NOR-thern HEM-is-feer) The top half of Earth

**orbit** (OR-bit) To travel around another object in a single path in space

**planet** An object that travels around a star, such as our Sun, is round, and is strong enough to keep other objects out of its path

**revolution** (rev-o-LOO-shun) To turn or cause to turn about an axis or a center for one complete rotation or orbit

**rotates** To turn about a center point or an axis

**solar system** (SOH-lur SIS-tum) The system made up of our Sun, the eight planets, moons, and other space objects

**southern hemisphere** (SU-thern HEM-is-feer) The bottom half of Earth

**telescope** (TEH-leh-skohp) An instrument used to make distant objects appear closer and larger

# Index

asteroids 4
axis 6
dwarf planets 4
Earth 4–6, 8–10, 12–13, 21
gravity 4-5
Jupiter 16–17, 21
Mars 9, 14–16, 21

Mercury 8–9, 21
moons 8, 10, 13, 16, 18, 20
Neptune 16, 20–21
orbit 5–6, 8, 13, 20
Pluto 5
revolution 6, 13
rotation 6, 12

Saturn 16, 18–19, 21
solar system 5–6, 10, 12, 16, 18, 21
Sun 4–8, 11, 12, 20
Uranus 16, 20–21
Venus 9–11, 21